JOURNEYS

Reader's Notebook
Volume 1

Grade 1

Houghton Mifflin Harcourt

Contents

Listen for the Short *a* and *m* Sounds

✏️ Say each picture name. Listen for the short a sound. Write the letter a to show where you hear the short a sound.

1.	2.	3.
_ _ _ _ _ ▮	_ _ _ _ _ ▮	_ _ _ _ _ ▮

✏️ Say each picture name. Listen for the m sound. Write the letter m to show where you hear the sound for m.

4.	5.	6.
_ _ _ ▮ _ _ _	_ _ _ ▮ _ _ _	_ _ _ ▮ _ _ _

Name _____

Words to Know

✏️ Read the words in the box. Then read and finish the sentences.

Words to Know

am   I   to   like

_____

I am _____ .

_____

I like to _____ .

🖍️ Draw a picture to go with your sentences.

Listen for the *s*, *m*, and Short *a* Sounds

Say each picture name. Listen for the /s/ sound. Write the letter **s** to show where you hear the sound for **s**.

1.	2.	3.

Listen to each picture name. Listen for the sounds. Use the letters **s**, **a**, or **m** to write the picture name. Remember that a person's name begins with a capital letter.

4.	5.	6.
___ ___ t	___ ___ d	___ ___ ___

Words to Know

Read the words in the box. Then read the story.

> ### Words to Know
>
> a   see   the   I   to   like

I am Sam.

I see a ＿＿＿ .

I like the ＿＿＿ .

I see a ＿＿＿ .

I like the ＿＿＿ .

 Draw what will happen next in the story.

Listen for the *t*, *s*, *m*, and Short *a* Sounds

Say each picture name. Listen for the *t* sound. Write the letter **t** to show where you hear the sound for **t**.

1.	2.	3.

Listen to each picture name. Listen for the sounds. Use the letters **t**, **s**, **a**, or **m** to write the name.

4.	5.	6.
p		

Name _____

Words to Know

 Read the words in the box. Then read the story. Draw a line under the words that have short **a**.

Words to Know

we   go   I   a   see   like   to   the

I am Tam.

I am Sam.

We see a mat.

We like the mat.

We go to the mat.

Draw what Sam and Tam will do next.

Name _____

Listen for the c, t, m, and Short a Sounds

🖍 Say each picture name. Listen for the sounds in the name. Color the pictures that begin with the same sound as cat.

1.

✏ Listen to each picture name. Listen for the sounds. Use the letters **c**, **t**, **a**, or **m** to write the picture name.

2.

_ _ _
_ _ _ p

3.

_ _ _
_ _ n

4.

_ _ _
_ _ _

Name _____

Words to Know

✏️ Read the words in the box. Then read the story. Draw a line under the words that have short **a**.

Words to Know

is   are   we   go   I   a   see   like   to   the

We see Sam.

Sam is the cat.

Am I a cat?

Is Cam a cat?

We are the .

We like Sam.

We go to see Sam!

🖍 Draw what will happen next in the story.

High-Frequency Words

BTS8

Grade 1

Name _____

Letters and Sounds

 Trace and read the words. Draw a line from each word to its picture.

 mat ★

cat ★

sat ★

★

★

★

 Circle the words that rhyme with at.

(at)   cat   Tam   mat

Cam   Sam   am   sat

Words to Know

Read the words in the box. Then read the story.

Words to Know

> a   are   go   I   like   is   see   the   to   we

We are at the .

We see a cat.

The cat is a .

I like the cat.

We like to go to the .

Think about places that you like to visit. Write about and draw your ideas.

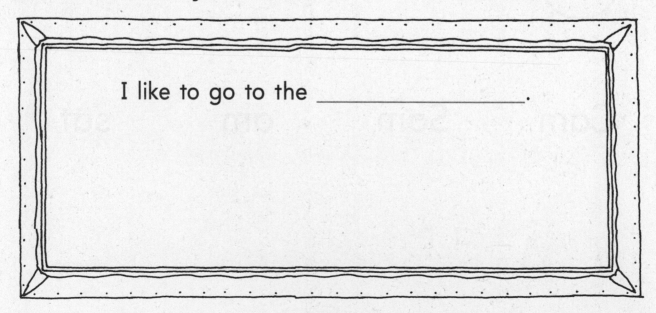

I like to go to the _____ .

Name _____

Words with Short *a*

 Write the missing letter. Read the word.

1.

___ a t

2.

___ a t

3.

D ___ n

4.

c ___ t

5.

___ a n

6.

S ___ m

Words to Know

🖉 Complete the sentences. Write a word from the box on each line.

Words to Know

with	help	and	you	play	be

1. Look at Cam _____ Sam.

2. What will this _____ ?

3. I like to _____ .

4. She can _____ .

5. Come _____ me, Sam!

6. _____ can go down.

Name _____

Consonants *s, n, d*

✏️ Name each picture. Think of the beginning sound. Write **s, n,** or **d**.

1.

_____
- - - - -
_____

2.

_____
- - - - -
_____

3.

- - - - -
_____

4.

- - - - -
_____

5.

_____
- - - - -
_____

6.

- - - - -
_____

Phonics

3

Grade 1, Unit 1

Name _____

Spelling Words with the Short *a* Sound

What Is a Pal?
Spelling: Words with Short *a*

✏️ Sort the words. Write the correct Spelling Words in each column.

Words that have 2 letters	Words that have 3 letters
_____	_____
- - - - - - - - - -	- - - - - - - - - -
_____	_____
- - - - - - - - - -	- - - - - - - - - -
_____	_____
- - - - - - - - - -	- - - - - - - - - -
_____	_____
- - - - - - - - - -	- - - - - - - - - -
_____	_____

Spelling Words

am
at
sat
man
dad
mat

Name _____

Nouns for People and Animals

🖉 Listen to the nouns in the Word Bank. Read along. Write nouns from the box to name the people and animals in the picture.

_____ _____
- - - - - - - - - - - - - - - - - -
_____ _____

_____ _____
- - - - - - - - - - - - - - - - - -
_____ _____

Giving Details

 Listen to the words in the Word Bank. Read along. Add two details to this picture of two pals. Then write labels that tell who and what.

```
_____                        _____
- - - - - - - - - -                      - - - - - - - - - -


_____                        _____
- - - - - - - - - -                      - - - - - - - - - -

        _____  _____
        - - - - - - - -    - - - - - - - -
        _____  _____
```

Word Bank

cap	bat	bike	boy
Sam	Tom	pads	play

Consonants *p, f*

 Name each picture. Think of the beginning sound. Write **p** or **f**.

1.

_____
- - - - - - -
_____

2.

_____
- - - - - - -
_____

3.

_____
- - - - - - -
_____

4.

_____
- - - - - - -
_____

5.

_____
- - - - - - -
_____

6.

_____
- - - - - - -
_____

7.
_____
- - - - - - -
_____

8.

_____
- - - - - - -
_____

9.
_____
- - - - - - -
_____

Reader's Guide

What Is a Pal?

Letters to Pals

Be a pal. Write letters to your pals.

Read pages 16–17. Find ideas in the words and pictures about how pals can help. Write a letter to a pal. Ask for help with something.

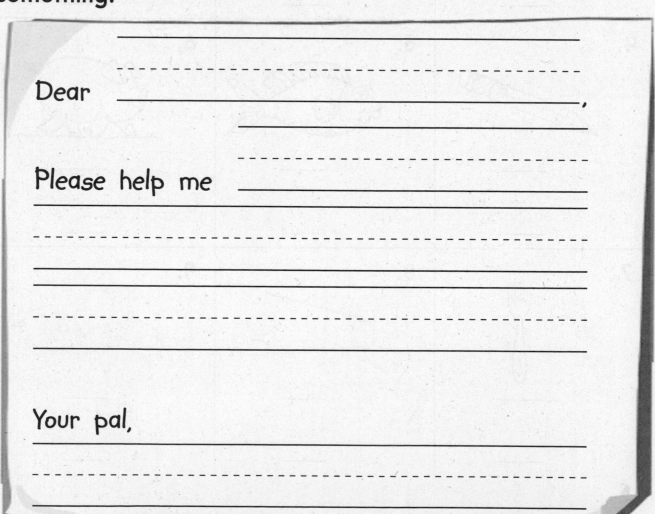

Dear _____,

_____

Please help me _____

_____

_____

_____

Your pal,

_____

Name _____ Date _____

Read pages 22–25. Find ideas in the selection about what pals do. What will you do with a pal? Write a letter. Draw a picture.

_____

- -

Dear _____,

_____

- -

Will you _____ with me?

Your pal,

_____

- -

_____

Spelling Words with the Short *a* Sound

✏️ Write the missing letter to complete each Spelling Word. Then write the word.

Spelling Words

am
at
sat
man
dad
mat

1. s ___ t _____

2. m ___ n _____

3. m ___ t _____

4. ___ t _____

5. d ___ d _____

6. ___ m _____

Name _____

Words That Name Places or Things

Listen to the nouns in the Word Bank. Read along. Write a noun from the box to name each picture.

Word Bank
- car
- rope
- park
- plate
- city

1.

_____
- - - - - - - - - - - - - -
_____

2.

_____
- - - - - - - - - - - - - -
_____

3.

_____
- - - - - - - - - - - - - -
_____

4.

_____
- - - - - - - - - - - - - -
_____

5.

_____
- - - - - - - - - - - - - -
_____

Name _____

Lesson 1
READER'S NOTEBOOK

My Pals

 Draw four pals. Show details that tell who, what, and where.

What Is a Pal?
Writing: Narrative Writing

My Pals

 Write labels for your pictures.

Spelling Words with the Short *a* Sound

Write the correct word to complete each sentence.

_____

1. This _____ is for the cat.   (mat, dad)

2. I _____ with it.   (dad, sat)

3. I _____ mad.   (mat, am)

4. Pat is _____ the play.   (at, am)

5. We like the _____.   (man, at)

6. We sat on _____.   (at, dad)

Spiral Review

✏️ Circle the correct word in each box to name each person and pet.

1.		sam / Sam
		al / Al
2.		Sal / sal
		Gam / gam
3.		dan / Dan
		cal / Cal
4.		Cam / cam
		Mag / mag

Grammar in Writing

Words that name people, animals, places, and
things are called **nouns**. Use nouns to name people,
animals, places, and things when you write.

The <u>boy</u> smiles.
The <u>dog</u> runs.
The <u>stick</u> flies.
The <u>park</u> is fun.

✏️ **Listen to the nouns in the Word Bank,
and to the sentences. Read along. Look at
the picture. Write nouns from the box to
finish the sentences.**

Word Bank

food
girl
cat
yard

1. The _____ plays.

2. The _____ cooks.

3. The _____ is crowded.

4. The _____ sleeps.

Words with Short *i*

 Write the missing letter. Read the word.

1.

s __ t

2.

T __ m

3.

p __ n

4.

f __ n

5.

s __ p

6.

h __ t

Words to Know

 Complete the sentences. Write a word from the box on each line.

Words to Know

he   look   have   too   for   what

_____

- - - - - - - - - - - - - - - - -

1. I will _____ for the cat.

_____

- - - - - - - - - - - - - - - - -

2. _____ is a good cat.

_____

- - - - - - - - - - - - - - - - -

3. My dad will look, _____ .

_____

- - - - - - - - - - - - - - - - -

4. He will help me look _____ the cat.

_____

- - - - - - - - - - - - - - - - -

5. _____ is this?

_____

- - - - - - - - - - - - - - - - -

6. I _____ the cat!

Consonants *r*, *h*, /z/*s*

 Write the missing letter. Read the word.

1.

__ a m

2.

h i __

3.

__ a m

4.

__ a n

5.

__ i p

6.

__ a t

Spelling Words with the Short *i* Sound

Sort the words. Write the correct Spelling Words in each column.

Spelling Words

if

is

him

rip

fit

pin

Words that have 2 letters	Words that have 3 letters
_____	_____
- - - - - - - -	- - - - - - - -
_____	_____
_____	_____
- - - - - - - -	- - - - - - - -
_____	_____
_____	_____
- - - - - - - -	- - - - - - - -
_____	_____
_____	_____
- - - - - - - -	- - - - - - - -
_____	_____

19

Name _____

Words That Show Ownership

✏️ Listen to the possessive nouns in the Word Bank. Read along. Write a possessive noun from the bank to name each picture.

Word Bank

boy's   man's   hen's   cat's

1. one _____ bag

2. a _____ dish

3. one _____ nest

4. a _____ glove

Name _____

Details

 Listen to the words in the Word Bank. Read along. Fill in each line to write captions for the picture. Choose words from the Word Bank or use your own.

Word Bank

vests
paddles
river
boat
flowers

_____

Mac is in the _____ .

_____

Ma and Dad have _____

_____

We will _____ .

Name _____

Consonants *b, g*

Name each picture. Think of the ending
sound. Write **b** or **g**.

1.

_ _ _ _ _ _
_____

2.

_ _ _ _ _ _
_____

3.

_ _ _ _ _ _
_____

4.

_ _ _ _ _ _
_____

5.

_ _ _ _ _ _
_____

6.

_ _ _ _ _ _
_____

Reader's Guide

The Storm

A Dog's Story

My pal Rip spent time in a storm.

Read pages 48–49. Help Rip tell his pal Skip about the storm.

First, Tim and I went to _____ .

Next, we saw _____ .

I felt _____ .

Read pages 50–53. Tell how Pop helps Tim and Rip.

_____

- - - - - - - - - - - - - - - - - - -

Pop gave Tim _____

_____

- - - - - - - - - - - - - - - - - - -

_____ .

_____

- - - - - - - - - - - - - - - - - - -

Pop gave me _____ .

_____

- - - - - - - - - - - - - - - - - - -

I felt _____ .

_____

- - - - - - - - - - - - - - - - - - -

Then Pop sat and read. We _____

_____

- - - - - - - - - - - - - - - - - - -

_____ .

Spelling Words with the Short *i* Sound

Write the missing letter to complete each Spelling Word. Then write the word.

Spelling Words

if
is
him
rip
fit
pin

1. f ___ t _____

2. p ___ n _____

3. r ___ p _____

4. ___ f _____

5. h ___ m _____

6. ___ s _____

Words That Show Ownership

Listen to the possessive nouns in the Word Bank. Read along. Write a possessive noun from the bank to name each picture.

Word Bank

man's   cat's   bird's   girl's

1. a _____ tail

2. the _____ doll

3. a _____ glasses

4. the _____ nest

Planning My Caption

 Draw a picture of your family in a favorite place.

My Family

 Write captions that tell about your picture.

_____

- -

_____

_____

- -

_____

_____

- -

_____

Spelling Words with the Short *i* Sound

✏️ **Write the correct word to complete each sentence.**

_____

1. We play with _____ .   (is, him)

_____

2. What did you _____ ?   (rip, if)

_____

3. Kip _____ a pal.   (is, him)

_____

4. Do you have a _____ ?   (pin, him)

_____

5. Can the hat _____ ?   (pin, fit)

_____

6. Will you play _____ I do?   (fit, if)

Name _____

Spiral Review

✏️ Draw a line under the nouns in each sentence.

1. The dog is under the bed.

2. Our house is near the school.

3. The girl and boy are reading.

4. One bird is in that tree.

5. That man lives in the city.

Grammar in Writing

Words that show that one person or animal has or owns something are called **possessive nouns**. Use possessive nouns to show ownership when you write.

The <u>man's</u> scarf is warm.

✏️ Listen to the possessive nouns in the Word Bank. Read along. Write a possessive noun from the bank in the sentence about each picture.

Word Bank

cat's

boy's

girl's

dog's

1. The _____ bike is new.

2. The _____ hat is big

3. The _____ bed looks soft.

4. The _____ tail is long.

Words with Short o

Curious George at School
Phonics: Short o

 Name each picture. Color the pictures with short **o**.

Name _____

Lesson 3
READER'S NOTEBOOK

Curious George
at School
High-Frequency Words

Words to Know

Complete the sentences. Write a word from the box on each line.

Words to Know

do   find   funny   sing   no   they

_____

1. Look at the _____ cat!

_____

2. _____ like to help.

_____

3. What will he _____ now?

_____

4. Dan will _____ now.

_____

5. _____, he did not see the cat.

_____

6. We can _____ a mat for you.

32

Name _____

Consonants *l, x*

✏️ Finish the rhymes. Write one of the
words from the box on the line.

six   box

Look at the fox.

_____ _____

- - - - - - - - - - -

It is on the _____ _____ _____ .

lot   log

Bob did not jog.

_____ _____

- - - - - - - - - - -

Bob sat on a _____ _____ _____ .

33

Spelling Words with the Short *o* Sound

✏️ Sort the words. Write the correct Spelling Words in each column.

Words that rhyme	Words that do not rhyme
_____	_____
_____	_____
_____	_____
_____	_____
_____	_____

Spelling Words

log

dot

top

hot

lot

ox

Name _____

Action Verbs

✏️ Listen to the verbs in the Word Bank. Read along. Write verbs from the box to tell about the actions in the pictures.

Word Bank

eat
run
drink
draw

1. _____

2. _____

3. _____

4. _____

Purpose

Draw two people at school. Show each one doing something different.

Listen to the words in the box. Read along. Write two sentences about your pictures. Tell what each person is doing.

Who	**Action Verb**	**Exact Noun**

Who	**Action Verb**	**Exact Noun**

| ball | book | drum | fish | games |
| paper | piano | picture | song | teacher |

Name _____

Lesson 3
READER'S NOTEBOOK

Curious George
at School
Phonics: Inflection -s

Words with Inflection -s

✏️ Name each picture. Write the word. Use words in the box.

sits	digs	pats	sips	bats	mops

1.

_____

- - - - - - - - - - - - - - -

_____

2.

_____

- - - - - - - - - - - - - - -

_____

3.

_____

- - - - - - - - - - - - - - -

_____

4.

_____

- - - - - - - - - - - - - - -

_____

5.

_____

- - - - - - - - - - - - - - -

_____

6.

_____

- - - - - - - - - - - - - - -

_____

Name _____ Date _____

Lesson 3
READER'S NOTEBOOK

Curious George at
School
Independent Reading

Curious George Goes to School

A Day at School

Hi! I am in Mr. Apple's class. Today, a monkey came to my school!

Read pages 72–74. Write what happened at school.

Curious George came to school. I had fun with George

- -

when we _____.

- -

_____.

- -

_____.

Name _____ Date _____

Lesson 3
READER'S NOTEBOOK

Curious George at
School
Independent Reading

Read pages 75–81.

George made a big mess. It looked _____

_____

_____

_____ .

George needed help. I helped by _____

_____

_____

_____ .

I want George to come back because _____

_____

_____

_____

_____

Name _____

Spelling Words with the Short *o* Sound

✏️ Write the missing letter to complete each Spelling Word. Then write the word.

log
dot
hot
top
lot
ox

1. l ___ t _____

2. l ___ g _____

3. h ___ t _____

4. ___ x _____

5. t ___ p _____

6. d ___ t _____

More Words That Show Action

✏️ Listen to the verbs in the Word Bank. Read along. Write a verb from the box to name each action in the picture.

Word Bank

climb
slide
jump
swing
throw

_____   _____
- - - - - - - - - - - - -   - - - - - - - - - - - - -
_____   _____

_____   _____
- - - - - - - - - - - - -   - - - - - - - - - - - - -
_____   _____

_____
- - - - - - - - - - - - -
_____

Planning My Sentences

✏️ Write an action verb at the top of each box. Draw a picture to go with the verb.

Spelling Words with the Short *o* Sound

✏️ Write the correct word to complete each sentence.

_____

1. A _____ is not big.   (hot, dot)

_____

2. The _____ is big.   (log, hot)

_____

3. We have a _____ of cats.   (lot, top)

_____

4. Pam is at the _____ .   (dog, top)

_____

5. Do you have a _____ pot?   (hot, log)

_____

6. Did you ever see an _____ ?   (ox, hot)

Spiral Review

 Circle the possessive noun that shows ownership. Then write the possessive noun.

1. A boy's bike is in the yard.

_____

- - - - - - - - - - - - - - - - - -

_____

2. The cat's food is in the dish.

_____

- - - - - - - - - - - - - - - - - -

_____

3. The man's car is red.

_____

- - - - - - - - - - - - - - - - - -

_____

4. That ball is the dog's toy.

_____

- - - - - - - - - - - - - - - - - -

_____

5. A girl's map is over there.

_____

- - - - - - - - - - - - - - - - - -

_____

Grammar in Writing

Words that tell what people and animals do are called **verbs**.

They <u>run</u> on the playground.

✏️ **Circle the verb to finish each sentence. Write the verb on the line.**

_____
- - - - - - - - - - - - - - - - - -

1. Sal can _____ with a bat.

        hit   **fit**

_____
- - - - - - - - - - - - - - - - - -

2. They _____ big bags.

      make   **sit**

_____
- - - - - - - - - - - - - - - - - -

3. We _____ the dogs.

     go   **see**

_____
- - - - - - - - - - - - - - - - - -

4. Bob and Meg _____ a cat.

      find   **hop**

Name _____

Words with Short *e*

✏️ Circle the word that matches each picture.

1.

win   web

2.

mat   men

3.

net   can

4.

pen   pin

5.

ten   tin

6.

bad   bed

Name _____

Words to Know

✏️ Complete the sentences. Write a word from the box on each line.

Words to Know

all	does	here	me	my	who

_____

- -

1. Lin is _____ pal.

_____

- -

2. Sam will come _____ to play.

_____

- -

3. He likes to play with _____ .

_____

- -

4. I will see _____ is there.

_____

- -

5. Sam _____ a funny trick.

_____

- -

6. We will take up _____ the mats.

Consonants *y, w*

✏️ Name each picture. Think of the beginning sound. Write **y** or **w**.

1.

_____

2.

_____

3.

_____

4.

_____

5.

_____

6.

_____

Spelling Words with the Short *e* Sound

Sort the words. Write the correct Spelling Words in each column.

Words that rhyme with **get**	Words that rhyme with **den**	Words that do not rhyme
_____	_____	_____
_____	_____	_____
_____	_____	_____

Spelling Words

yet

web

pen

wet

leg

hen

Name _____

Adjectives for Size

Listen to the adjectives. Read along. Circle the adjective that describes what the picture shows. Write the adjective.

1.

small

big

2.

long

short

3.

narrow

wide

4.

short

tall

Using Words That Are Just Right

🖊 Cross out the word that is the same in each sentence. Listen to the words in the box. Read along. Write a better word from the box.

> **Word Bank**
>
> | busy | large | new | sweet |
> |------|-------|-----|-------|
> | round | kind | square | tall |

_____

1. Our town has a good market. _____

2. Mom and I get good apples there. _____

3. We got a good cake for Dad. _____

4. The man that helps us is good. _____

Consonants *k, v, j*

Lucia's Neighborhood
Phonics: Consonants *k, v, j*

✏️ Name each picture. Think of the beginning sound. Write **k, v,** or **j.**

1.

_____
_ _ _ _ _

2.

_____
_ _ _ _ _

3.

_____
_ _ _ _ _

4.

_____
_ _ _ _ _

5.

_____
_ _ _ _ _

6.

_____
_ _ _ _ _

7.

_____
_ _ _ _ _

8.

_____
_ _ _ _ _

9.

_____
_ _ _ _ _

Reader's Guide

Lucia's Neighborhood

Lucia's Map

Lucia's uncle is coming to visit! Draw a map to help him find her.

Read pages 100–105 again. Draw where each place is. Write the place name.

Read pages 106–109. Make another map for this part of the story. Draw where each place is. Write the place name.

Name _____

Spelling Words with the Short *e* Sound

✏️ Write the missing letter to complete each Spelling Word. Then write the word.

Spelling Words

yet
web
pen
wet
leg
hen

1. y ___ t _____

2. h ___ n _____

3. w ___ b _____

4. l ___ g _____

5. p ___ n _____

6. w ___ t _____

Name _____

Adjectives for Shape

 Listen to and follow the directions.

1. Circle the shape that is **round**.

2. Circle the shape that is **flat**.

3. Circle the shape that is **square**.

4. Circle the shape that is **curved**.

Name _____

Spelling Words with the Short *e* Sound

✏️ Write the correct word to complete each sentence.

1. He is not here _____ . (yet, web)

2. The _____ is big. (wet, hen)

3. My _____ is red. (pen, wet)

4. The dog is all _____ . (wet, hen)

5. I can hop on my _____ . (yet, leg)

6. I can see a _____ . (wet, web)

Spiral Review

Listen to the verbs in the Word Bank. Read along. Write verbs from the bank to tell about the actions in the pictures.

Word Bank

hop
dig
read
swim

1. _____

2. _____

3. _____

4. _____

Grammar in Writing

Words that describe people, animals, or things are called **adjectives**. Adjectives can describe size or shape.

> The house is <u>big</u>. (size)
> The truck is <u>wide</u>. (shape)

 Listen to the adjectives in the Word Banks. Read along. Write on the line an adjective for size.

_____

1. A leg is _____ .

_____

2. A dot is _____ .

Word Bank

long

little

 Write on the line an adjective for shape.

_____

3. A map is _____ .

_____

4. A log is _____ .

Word Bank

flat

round

Name _____

Words with Short *u*

 Write the missing letter. Read the word.

1.

__

p __ p

2.

__

c __ p

3.

__

m __ d

4.

__

t __ b

5.

__

f __ n

6.

__

__ p

Words to Know

✏️ Draw a line to the word that completes the sentence. Write the word on the line.

_____

1. Tom will _____ the sled.　　　　　**hold**

2. It was _____ to sit for a bit.　　　　**full**

3. All the bags are _____ .　　　　　　**pull**

4. Mel has _____ pals.　　　　　　　**friend**

5. Cam is my _____ .　　　　　　　**good**

6. Mom will _____ my books for me.　　**many**

　　　　61

More Words with Short *u*

 Write the missing letter. Read the word.

1.

_____
- - - -
___ u g

2.

_____
- - - -
___ u n

3.

_____
- - - -
___ u s

4.

_____
- - - -
___ u t

5.

_____
- - - -
___ u g

6.

_____
- - - -
___ u n

Spelling Words with the Short *u* Sound

Sort the words. Write the correct Spelling Words in each column.

Words that rhyme	Words that do not rhyme

Spelling Words

up
bug
mud
nut
hug
tub

Name _____

Adjectives for Color

Listen to the directions. Read along.
Color each picture.

1. Color the cap **blue**.

2. Color the toy **yellow**.

3. Color the ball **orange**.

4. Color the apple **red**.

5. Color the bug **black**.

Telling More

 Write each sentence. Choose an
adjective from the box to tell more.

big	many	ten	mad
bad	good	red	tan
sad	funny	hot	wet

1. Dad and I get on a bus.

_____

- - - - - - - - - - - - - - - -

Dad and I get on a _____ bus.

2. We go to a park.

_____

- - - - - - - - - - - - - - - -

We go to a _____ park.

3. We see a man with pets.

_____

- - - - - - - - - - - - - - - -

We see a man with _____ pets.

4. Dad gets me a hat!

_____

- - - - - - - - - - - - - - - -

Dad gets me a _____ hat!

Consonants *qu*, *z*

✏️ Name each picture. Think of the beginning sound. Write **qu** or **z**.

1.

_____
_ _ _ _ _ _ _
_____

2.

_____
_ _ _ _ _ _ _
_____

3.

_____
_ _ _ _ _ _ _
_____

4.

_____
_ _ _ _ _ _ _
_____

5.

_____
_ _ _ _ _ _ _
_____

6.

_____
_ _ _ _ _ _ _
_____

Reader's Guide

Gus Takes the Train

Gus's Trip

Read pages 128–132. Gus needs a ticket to get on the train. A ticket tells the conductor many things.

Draw a ticket for Gus. Write his name, where he is going, and what he is bringing with him.

Name _____ Date _____

Read pages 133–137. Gus meets a friend. Gus draws and writes in his journal. Draw the two friends on the train. Write about what they do.

 Gus's Journal

Friends

_____

- -

_____

_____

- -

_____

Name _____

Spelling Words with the Short *u* Sound

Gus Takes the Train
Spelling: Words with Short *u*

 Write the missing letter to complete each Spelling Word. Then write the word.

Spelling Words

up
bug
mud
nut
hug
tub

____
- - - - -
1. n ___ t
____

2. b ___ g
____

- - - - -
3. m ___ d
____

- - - - -
4. ___ p
____

- - - - -
5. t ___ b
____

- - - - -
6. h ___ g

Adjectives for Number

 Listen to the adjectives in the Word Bank. Read along. Write a word from the box to describe each picture.

Word Bank

two   three   four   six

1.

_____

- - - - - - - - - - - - - - -

_____

2.

_____

- - - - - - - - - - - - - - -

_____

3.

_____

- - - - - - - - - - - - - - -

_____

4.

_____

- - - - - - - - - - - - - - -

_____

Name _____

Spelling Words with the Short *u* Sound

Write the correct word to complete each sentence.

_____

- - - - - - - - - - - - - - - - -

1. Dad likes to _____ the cat.   (up, hug)

_____

- - - - - - - - - - - - - - - -

2. A _____ is on my leg!   (bug, hug)

_____

- - - - - - - - - - - - - - - - -

3. Put the mat _____ on top.   (nut, up)

_____

- - - - - - - - - - - - - - - -

4. I got wet in the _____ .   (tub, bug)

_____

- - - - - - - - - - - - - - - -

5. Do you have a _____ for me?   (nut, mud)

_____

- - - - - - - - - - - - - - - -

6. The pig likes to play in the _____ .
   (mud, hug)

Spiral Review

✏️ Listen to the adjectives in the Word Bank. Read along. Write an adjective from the Bank to tell about each picture.

1.   The hoop is _____
   _ _ _ _ _ _ _ _ _ _ _ _ _
   _____.

2.   The ant is _____
   _ _ _ _ _ _ _ _ _ _ _ _ _
   _____.

3.   The rope is _____
   _ _ _ _ _ _ _ _ _ _ _ _ _
   _____.

4. [window image]   The window is _____
   _ _ _ _ _ _ _ _ _ _ _ _ _
   _____.

Name _____

Grammar in Writing

Words that describe people, places, animals, or things are called **adjectives**. Adjectives can describe color and number.

   The train is <u>black</u>. The <u>five</u> seats are <u>red</u>.

✏️ **Finish each sentence with an adjective for number. Use the Word Bank.**

Word Bank

one

three

_____

1. I see _____ flowers.

_____

2. I see _____ cat.

🖍️ **Listen to and follow the directions.**

3. Draw **two** apples.
   Color the apples **red**.

4. Draw **four** bugs.
   Color the bugs **black**.

Lesson 6
READER'S NOTEBOOK

Jack and the Wolf
Phonics: Double Final
Consonants and *ck*

Name _____

Double Final Consonants and *ck*

✏️ Name each picture. Write the letters from the box that stand for the ending sound.

ck gg ss ll

1.

q u a _ _ _

2.

h i _ _ _

3.

l o _ _ _

4.

e _ _ _

5.

d o _ _ _

6.

s o _ _ _

Name _____

Words to Know

 Fill in the blanks to complete the sentences.
Write a word from the box on each line.

Words to Know

hear   call   come

said   every   away

_____

- - - - - - - - - - - - - - -

1. Does _____ dog like to play?

_____

- - - - - - - - - - - - - - -

2. Mem _____ she did not see the dog.

_____

- - - - - - - - - - - - - - -

3. Jack will _____ to help me.

_____

- - - - - - - - - - - - - - -

4. Sam and Jill are far _____ .

_____

- - - - - - - - - - - - - - -

5. Did you _____ the clock tick?

_____

- - - - - - - - - - - - - - -

6. Von will _____ on me to sing.

Double Final Consonants and *ck*

✏️ Circle the letters to make the word that matches the picture. Write the letters.

1.

b u _ _ _ _

ck   zz

2.

t a _ _ _ _

ss   ck

3.

p u _ _ _

gg   ff

4.

m i _ _ _

ss   tt

5.

h i _ _ _

ss   ll

6.

d u _ _ _

ll   ck

Spelling Words with the Short *a* Sound

Sort the words. Write the correct Spelling Words in each column.

Spelling Words

an
bad
can
had
cat
ran

Words that begin with a vowel	Words that begin with a consonant
_____	_____
_____	_____
_____	_____
_____	_____
_____	_____
_____	_____

What Is a Sentence?

Jack and the Wolf
Grammar: Complete Sentences

 Draw a line under each sentence.

1. The friends play.

2. a cat

3. The dog runs.

4. sit

 Draw lines to make sentences.

5. The hen   sits on a rock.

6. Gram   like to sing.

7. Jack   sits on eggs.

8. We   makes a doll.

Using Sense Words

deep
hot
loud
small
soft
sunny
sweet
warm

Listen to the sense words in the box and the sentences below. Read along. Write words from the box to finish the sentences about the picture.

_____

1. The bananas smell _____ .

2. The lion's fur feels _____ .

3. The seal's bark sounds _____ .

4. The monkeys look _____ .

Short *a*, Double Final Consonants, and *ck*

✏️ Name each picture. Write words from the box.

| fill | wag | yam | quick | van | neck |

1.

_____

- - - - - - - - - - -

_____

2.

_____

- - - - - - - - - - -

_____

3.

_____

- - - - - - - - - - -

_____

4.

_____

- - - - - - - - - - -

_____

5.

_____

- - - - - - - - - - -

_____

6.

_____

- - - - - - - - - - -

_____

Jack and the Wolf

Jack's Rules

Jack has a job. He takes care of the sheep.

Read pages 16–17. What does Jack do?

What rules is he following?

Rules for Jack

1. _____
   _____.

2. _____
   _____.

3. _____
   _____.

Read pages 18–29. Jack learns a lesson. Write more rules Jack will follow to do his job better.

4. _____
_____
_____.

5. _____
_____
_____.

6. _____
_____
_____.

Spelling Words with the Short *a* Sound

Spelling Words
an
bad
can
had
cat
ran

✏️ Write the Spelling Words that rhyme with **man**.

1. _____

2. _____

3. _____

✏️ Write the Spelling Words that rhyme with **dad**.

4. _____   5. _____

✏️ Write the Spelling Word that rhymes with **sat**.

6. _____

Is It a Sentence?

Jack and the Wolf
Grammar: Complete Sentences

 Draw a line under each sentence.

1. The dog naps.

naps

2. Tim and Jim

Tim and Jim run away.

3. the friends

The friends come to help.

4. The man sits down.

sits

5. sings

He sings.

6. get up

The dog will get up.

Grammar
84
Grade 1, Unit 2

Planning My Sentences

✏️ Listen to the labels in the web and read along. Write and draw details that describe your topic. You do not have to write words for every sense.

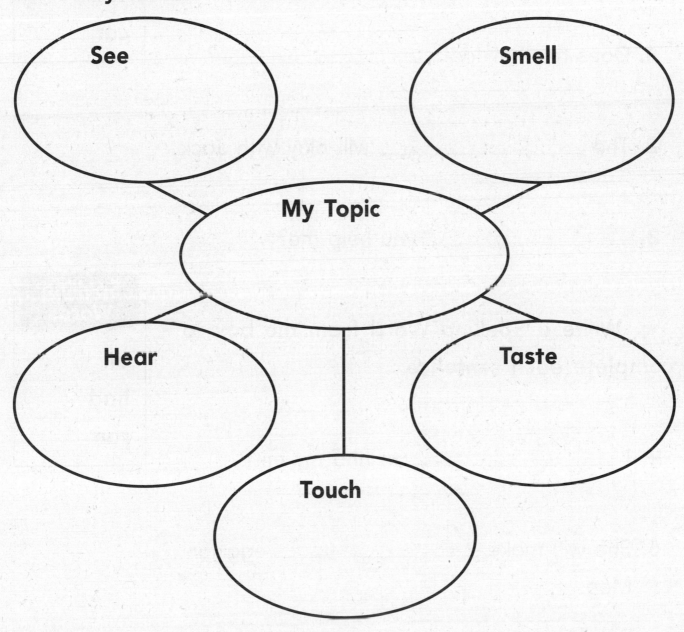

See

Smell

My Topic

Hear

Taste

Touch

Spelling Words with the Short *a* Sound

 Write a Spelling Word from the box to complete each sentence.

_____

- - - - - - - - - - - - - - - - - -

1. Does this hat look _____ ?

_____

- - - - - - - - - - - - - - - -

2. The _____ will play with Jack.

_____

- - - - - - - - - - - - - - - -

3. _____ you help me?

 Write a Spelling Word from the box to complete each sentence.

_____

- - - - - - - - - - - - - - - -

4. I _____ to find my mitt.

_____

- - - - - - - - - - - - - - - -

5. She will make _____ egg for Meg.

_____

- - - - - - - - - - - - - - - -

6. I _____ out to play.

Spiral Review

 Listen to the adjectives in the Word
Bank. Read along. Write a word from
the bank to tell about each picture.

Word Bank

three

six

four

1. I see _____ balls.

2. I see _____ birds.

3. I see _____ pears.

 Listen to and follow the directions.

4. Draw two bananas.
   Color the bananas yellow.

5. Draw five nuts.
   Color the nuts brown.

Grammar in Writing

A **sentence** is a group of words. A sentence tells who or what. It also tells what someone or something does or did.

Sentence	Not a Sentence
All the ducks sit.	sit
	all the ducks

✏️ Circle the two groups of words that are not sentences.

1. We have fun.

3. The dog runs away.

2. get mad

4. Jack

✏️ Add words to make the word groups you circled complete sentences. Write the new sentences.

5. _____

_____

6. _____

Name _____

Blends with *r*

Name each picture. Write letters from the box to complete the word.

br	cr	dr	gr	tr

1.

___ ___ i n

2.

___ ___ i m

3.

___ ___ i p

4.

___ ___ i b

5.

___ ___ i p

6.

___ ___ i m

Name _____

Lesson 7
READER'S NOTEBOOK

How Animals
Communicate
High-Frequency Words

Words to Know

 Fill in the blanks to complete the sentences.

> **Words to Know**
>
> | animal | why | how |
> |---|---|---|
> | some | make | of |

1. Tell me _____ you like to sing.

2. The bug can _____ a hut out of mud!

3. Bob will go with _____ friends.

4. He can tell you _____ to bat.

5. Six _____ the bags are full.

6. What _____ do you have as a pet?

**How Animals
Communicate**
Phonics: Blends with *r*

Blends with *r*

✏️ Name each picture. Circle the letters that stand for the beginning sounds. Write the letters to make the word.

1.

   fr   cr

   ___ ___ a b

2.

   pr   tr

   ___ ___ a p

3.

   pr   fr

   ___ ___ o g

4.

   gr   pr

   ___ ___ i l l

5.

   dr   gr

   ___ ___ u m

6.

   gr   br

   ___ ___ i c k

Spelling Words with the Short *i* Sound

Sort the words. Write the correct Spelling Words in each column.

Spelling Words

in
will
did
sit
six
big

Words that begin with a vowel	Words that begin with a consonant
_____	_____
_____	_____
_____	_____
_____	_____
_____	_____
_____	_____
_____	_____
_____	_____
_____	_____
_____	_____

Name _____

Commas in a Series

✏️ Listen to each sentence. Read along.
Add commas where they belong.

1. They had dogs hens   chicks.

2. Cats dogs   fish are pets.

3. My dog can sit beg   run.

4. I saw frogs bugs   fish.

5. A bull kicks jumps   runs.

Name _____

Lesson 7
READER'S NOTEBOOK

How Animals
Communicate
Writing: Informative Writing

Adjectives

 Draw a picture of an animal doing something.

big
small
slow
loud
quiet
soft
young

Listen to the adjectives in the Word Bank. Read along. Complete each sentence with a word from the Word Bank or your own adjective.

_____

1. The animal is _____ .

_____

2. The animal is _____ .

_____

3. The animal is _____ .

_____

4. The animal is _____ .

Short *i* and Blends with *r*

Write words that rhyme. Use the words in the box.

trick grab dress drill grass quit tracks truck

1. brick

2. grill

3. press

4. crab

5. cracks

6. duck

7. sit

8. brass

Name _____ Date _____

Lesson 7
READER'S NOTEBOOK

How Animals
Communicate
Independent Reading

 Reader's Guide

How Animals Communicate

Make a Chart

You read about animal senses. Make a chart to show what you know.

Read pages 48–53. Fill in the chart.

This is a _____ .	I hear a _____ .
This is a _____ .	I hear a _____ .

What communication do you hear right now?

_____

_____

Read pages 54–61. Fill in the chart.

This is a
_____
_ _ _ _ _ _ _ _ _ _
_____ .

I see the dog
_____
_ _ _ _ _ _ _ _ _ _
_____ .

This is a
_____
_ _ _ _ _ _ _ _ _ _
_____ .

I see the bee
_____
_ _ _ _ _ _ _ _ _ _
_____ .

How are you using your eyes to communicate right now?

_____

- -

_____

- -

_____

- -

_____

- -

_____

Spelling Words with the Short *i* Sound

 Circle the Spelling Word that names the picture. Then write the word.

Spelling Words

in
will
did
sit
six
big

1. six
sip

_____

- - - - - - - - - - - - - -

_____

2. pin
in

_____

- - - - - - - - - - - - - -

_____

3. fit
sit

_____

- - - - - - - - - - - - - -

_____

4. big
bag

_____

- - - - - - - - - - - - - -

_____

 Write a Spelling Word that rhymes with each word below.

_____

- - - - - - - - - - - - - -

5. hid
_____

- - - - - - - - - - - - - -

6. fill
_____

Commas in a Series

Read each list of words. Write a sentence that uses the words in a list. Use commas and the word <u>and</u> where they belong.

sit	run	beg

_____

1. My dog can _____.

sing	read	draw

_____

2. I like to _____.

hop	swim	eat

_____

3. A frog can _____.

run	play	nap

_____

4. A cat can _____.

Planning My Poem

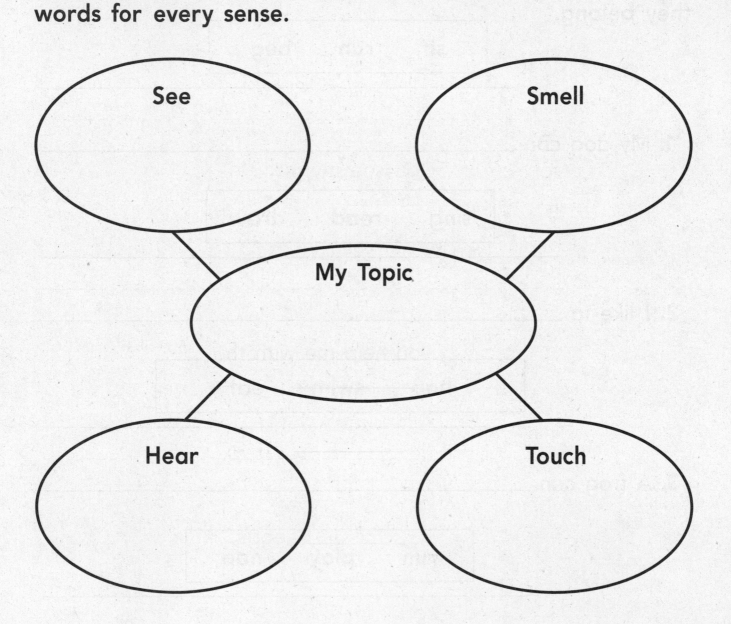 Write and draw details that describe your topic. Listen to the names of the senses and read along. You do not have to write words for every sense.

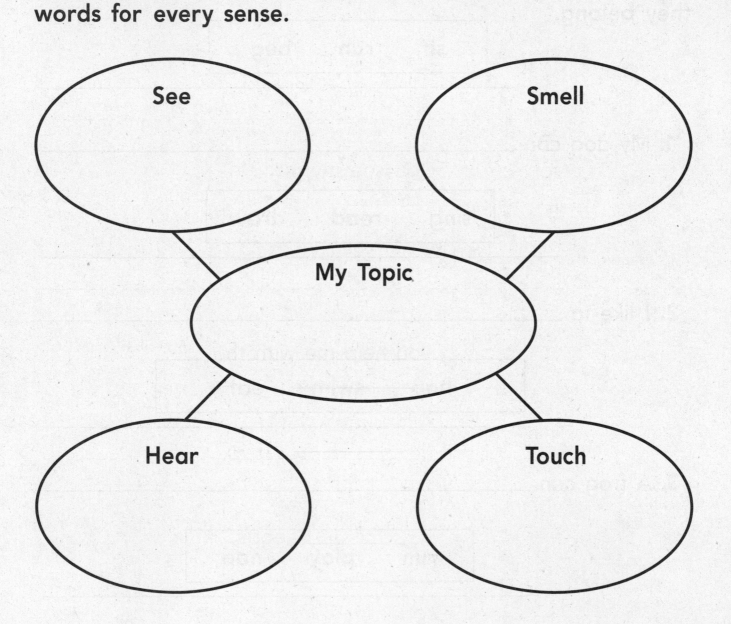

Spelling Words with the Short *i* Sound

✏️ Write the correct word to complete each sentence.

_____

- - - - - - - - - - - - - - -

1. I have a _____ dog. (big, bag)

_____

- - - - - - - - - - - - - - -

2. _____ you see my mat? (Dad, Did)

_____

- - - - - - - - - - - - - - -

3. Jon will _____ down. (sit, sat)

_____

- - - - - - - - - - - - - - -

4. _____ you help me with the cats? (Wall, Will)

_____

- - - - - - - - - - - - - - -

5. I put the hat _____ my bag. (in, an)

_____

- - - - - - - - - - - - - - -

6. The hen has _____ eggs. (mix, six)

Name _____

Spiral Review

Listen to the nouns in the Word Bank. Read along. Write a noun from the box to name each picture.

Word Bank

girl
pond
cat
bowl

1. _____

2. _____

3. _____

4. _____

Grammar in Writing

A sentence with a list of three items will have a comma after each of the first two items. The word *and* is used before the last item.

 Example: I like red, blue, and green.

 Use each word group to write a complete sentence.

1. bread   butter   jam

_____

- -

_____.

2. walk   run   hop

_____

- -

_____.

3. cats   dogs   fish

_____

- -

_____.

A Musical Day
Phonics: Blends with l

Blends with l

 Name each picture. Write the first two letters to make the word.

1.

__ __ a t e

2.

__ __ a y

3.

__ __ o c k

4.

__ __ a d

5.

__ __ a t

6.

__ __ e d

Name _____

Words to Know

Choose the word that fits best in the sentence. Write the word on the line.

1. Jen will fix (her, she, today) bed.

_____

2. I (our, here, would) like to help.

_____

3. (Her, Now, She) is my friend.

_____

4. We have a lot to do (our, today, she).

_____

5. We did (she, here, our) job!

_____

6. We can play (our, now, her).

_____

Blends with *l*

 Circle the word to finish the sentence.
Write the word.

1.

_____

- - - - - - - - - -

She will _____ .

slip   slap

2.

_____

- - - - - - - - - -

This is a _____ .

clam   blot

3.

_____

- - - - - - - - - -

Who will _____ this?

slip   flip

4.

_____

- - - - - - - - - -

I have a _____ .

plan   blab

5.

_____

- - - - - - - - - -

This is a big _____ .

blot   flap

6.

_____

- - - - - - - - - -

He is _____ to play.

clap   glad

Spelling Words with the Short *o* Sound

Spelling Words

on
fox
got
hop
pop
not

 Write the Spelling Words that rhyme with **dot**.

1. _____

2. _____

 Write the Spelling Words that rhyme with **top**.

3. _____

4. _____

 Write the Spelling Word that rhymes with **ox**.

5. _____

 Write the Spelling Word that rhymes with **Don**.

6. _____

What Is a Statement?

✏️ Draw a line under each statement.

1. He makes a drum.

2. sings

3. She plays well.

4. Our band will win.

5. Bill and Sam

6. Nick claps for us.

✏️ Use a word from the box to make each group of words a statement.

Word Bank

listen

Meg

7. _____ plays the drums.

_____

8. Ken and Kim _____ .

Purpose

✏️ Fill in the blanks in the draft of the thank-you note. Listen to the adjectives in the Word Bank. Read along. Choose adjectives from the box to help show why you are thankful. Write your own words, too.

Word Bank

hot	huge	icy	tall	round
soft	striped	sweet	green	yellow

_____

_____

Dear _____ ,
_____

_____

Thank you for the _____
_____

_____ _____

_____ . It is _____

_____

_____ . I like the _____

_____

_____ _____ .

Name _____

Blends with *l*

✏️ Name each picture. Circle the letters that stand for the beginning sounds. Write the word.

1.

cr   gr

_____

- - - - - - - - - -

2.

fl   fr

_____

- - - - - - - - - -

3.

fl   sl

_____

- - - - - - - - - -

4.

br   dr

_____

- - - - - - - - - -

5.

gr   dr

_____

- - - - - - - - - -

6.

pl   bl

_____

- - - - - - - - - -

Reader's Guide

A Musical Day

How to Make a Band

Aunt Viv came over! We made a band.
Here are the steps.

Read pages 85–91. Look at the pictures.
Write how the girls make guitars.

First, _____
_____ .

↓

Next, _____ .

↓

Last, _____ .

Read pages 89–93 again. Look at the pictures. Write how the boys make drums.

First, _____ .

↓

Next, _____ .

↓

Last, _____ .

Spelling Words with the Short *o* Sound

✏️ Write the missing letter to complete each Spelling Word. Then write the word.

Spelling Words

on
got
fox
hop
pop
not

1. f ___ x _____

2. n ___ t _____

3. p ___ p _____

4. h ___ p _____

5. ___ n _____

6. g ___ t _____

Writing Statements

 Circle the capital letter that begins each statement and the period that ends it.

1. Clem likes my song.

2. She sings for her mom.

3. Her mom sings, too.

4. They like to sing.

Write each statement correctly.

5. tess has a drum set

_____

- -

_____

6. she plays it a lot

_____

- -

_____

Planning My Thank-You Note

I will write my thank-you note to

_____

- -

_____.

Draw a picture of what you are thankful for. Write some details for your note.

_____
- - - - - - - - - - - - -
_____

_____
- - - - - - - - - - - - -
_____

_____
- - - - - - - - - - - - -
_____

I am thankful for

_____
- - - - - - - - - - - - -
_____

_____
- - - - - - - - - - - - -
_____

_____
- - - - - - - - - - - - -
_____

Spelling Words with the Short *o* Sound

 Write a Spelling Word to complete each sentence.

Spelling Words

on
fox
got
pop
not
hop

1. This animal is a _____ .

2. I _____ a dog from Bob.

3. I like caps but _____ hats.

4. The bag will _____ if you fill it up.

5. The fox will _____ off the box.

6. Do not sit _____ the bed.

Spiral Review

 Listen to the verbs in the Word Bank.
Read along. Write a verb from the box to
name each action.

Word Bank

play

dance

sing

watch

1. _____

   - - - - - - - - - - - - - - - -

   _____

2. _____

   - - - - - - - - - - - - - - - -

   _____

3. _____

   - - - - - - - - - - - - - - - -

   _____

4. _____

   - - - - - - - - - - - - - - - -

   _____

Grammar in Writing

A statement begins with a **capital letter** and ends with a **period**.

✏️ Fix the mistakes in these statements. Use proofreading marks.

Example: we play the bells
≡   ∧

1. she hits a big drum

2. he holds a doll

3. they have big hats

4. we tap and sing

Proofreading Marks	
∧	add
≡	capital letter

Blends with *s*

✏️ Name each picture. Write the first two
or three letters that stand for the beginning
sounds. Use the letters from the box.

st	sw	sn	sk	str

1. _____

2. _____

3. _____

4. _____

5. _____

Name _____

Words to Know

✏️ Circle the word that fits in each sentence. Write that word on the line.

This is my cat.

1. I like to (read, after, was).

_____

2. The cat (after, was, draw) in his bed.

_____

3. I like to (after, was, draw) animals.

_____

4. Here are (writes, pictures, reads) of my cat.

_____

5. Now I will (was, after, write) to my dad.

_____

6. I will help you (after, draw, read) I call Brad.

_____

Blends with *s*

 Circle the word that finishes the sentence.
Write the word.

1.

_____
- - - - - - -

Ann can _____ well.

spell   swim

2.

_____
- - - - - - -

Who made this _____?

spill   snag

3.

_____
- - - - - - -

I _____ in the tub.

sniff   scrub

4.

_____
- - - - - - -

This cat is not _____!

small   scrap

5.

_____
- - - - - - -

Pam likes to _____.

strum   smell

6.

_____
- - - - - - -

Kim will get a _____.

spin   snack

Spelling Words with the Short *e* Sound

Dr. Seuss
Spelling: Words with Short *e*

 Circle the word that names the picture. Then write the word.

Spelling Words

yes

let

red

ten

bed

get

1. bad
   bed

_____

- - - - - - - - - - - -

2. ten
   tan

_____

- - - - - - - - - - - -

 Write the Spelling Words that rhyme with **wet**.

3. _____

4. _____

 Proofread each sentence. Circle the Spelling Word that is wrong. Write it correctly.

_____

- - - - - - - - - - - -

5. I have a rud pen.

_____

- - - - - - - - - - - -

6. I said yez.

_____

Name _____

One and
More Than One

🖉 Listen to the nouns and read along.
Circle the noun for each picture below. Then
write the nouns you circled.

1.   bird   birds   _____

2.   boy   boys   _____

3.   ball   balls   _____

4.   tree   trees   _____

5.   cake   cakes   _____

Dr. Seuss
Writing: Informative Writing

Telling How Things Look

 Draw a picture of an animal.

one
two
three
four
blue
red
yellow
big
small
round

Finish the sentences that describe your animal. Listen to the words in the box. You can use these and other words you choose.

_____   _____

1. The _____ looks _____.

_____   _____

2. Its _____ are _____.

_____   _____

3. It has _____ _____.

Short *e* and Blends with *s*

✏️ Name each picture. Circle the letters that stand for the beginning sounds. Write the letters. Write the word.

1. st
    sw
    ___ ___ i m _____

2. ru
    re
    ___ ___ s t _____

3. st
    sn
    ___ ___ a c k _____

4. ve
    ne
    ___ ___ s t _____

5. fl
    sl
    ___ ___ i p _____

6. de
    di
    ___ ___ s k _____

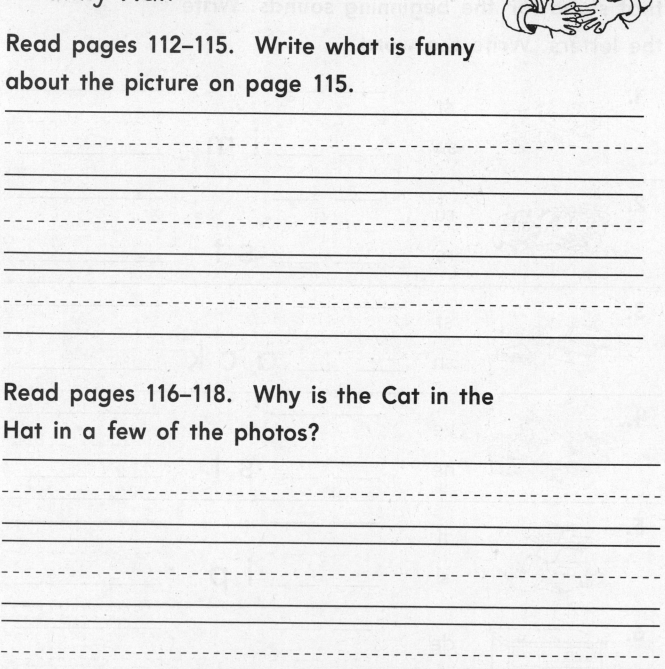

Dr. Seuss

A Funny Man

Read pages 112–115. Write what is funny about the picture on page 115.

_____

- -

_____

- -

_____

- -

_____

Read pages 116–118. Why is the Cat in the Hat in a few of the photos?

_____

- -

_____

- -

_____

- -

_____

Name _____ Date _____

Read pages 119–125. Now it's your turn to be funny! Ted wrote rhymes, and you can too. Write three words that rhyme. Write a funny sentence with your words.

_____

- -

_____

- -

_____.

Name _____

Spelling Words with the Short e Sound

Dr. Seuss
Spelling: Words with Short e

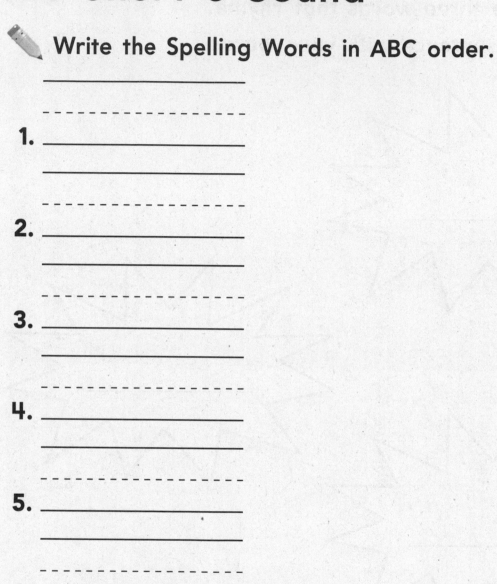 Write the Spelling Words in ABC order.

Spelling Words
yes
let
red
ten
bed
get

_____

1. _____

   _____

2. _____

   _____

3. _____

   _____

4. _____

   _____

5. _____

   _____

6. _____

Special Plural Nouns

✏️ Listen to the nouns and read along.
Circle the noun for each picture below. Then
write the nouns you circled. Complete the
sentences with the correct verb.

1.   woman   women   _____
   - - - - - - - - - - - - - - - -
   _____

2.   man   men   _____
   - - - - - - - - - - - - - - - -
   _____

3.   man   men   _____
   - - - - - - - - - - - - - - - -
   _____

4.   child   children   _____
   - - - - - - - - - - - - - - - -
   _____

_____
- - - - - - - - - - - - - - - -

5. The women _____ . (sing, sings)

_____
- - - - - - - - - - - - - - - -

6. The child _____ . (walk, walks)

Name _____

Spelling Words with the Short *e* Sound

Spelling Words

yes

let

red

ten

bed

get

Write a Spelling Word to complete each sentence.

_____

1. Get out of _____ , Fred!

2. Will you _____ me in?

3. Ben has _____ pet ducks.

4. Will you _____ that bug away from me?

5. _____ , I will hop with you.

6. Jeff likes the _____ cap best.

Name _____

Spiral Review

🖊 A complete sentence has two parts.
It tells who or what did something.
It also tells what someone or something
does or did.

who ⌒ what the cat does

The big black cat sits in the sun.

🖊 Draw a line under each group of words
that is a complete sentence.

1. My dog ate its food.

2. The bus came late.

3. eat lunch at school

4. the girls in my class

5. Our family went to the park.

131

Planning My Description

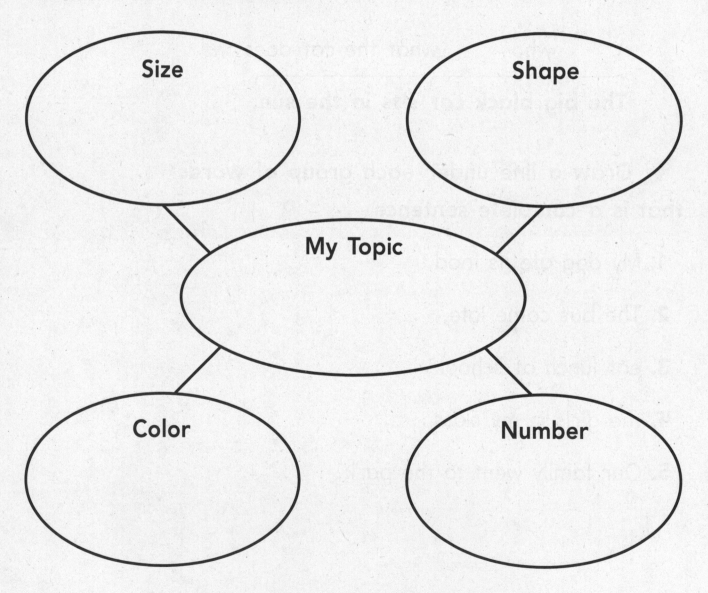 Listen to the labels in the web and read along. Write and draw details that tell size, shape, color, and number.

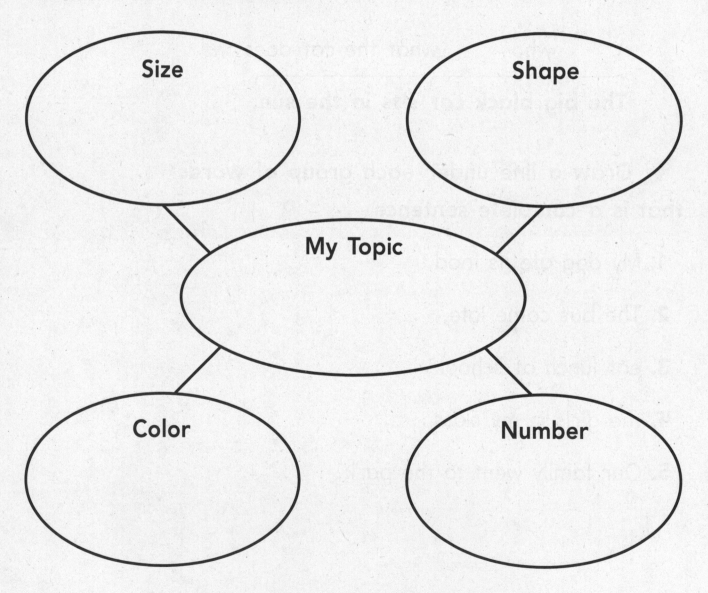

Grammar in Writing

Some **nouns** name **one.** Some nouns name **more than one.**

An **s** ending means more than one. Some special nouns change their spelling to name more than one.

Listen to the sentences and read along. Fix the mistakes in these statements. Use proofreading marks.

Examples: I read three ~~book.~~ **books** Two ~~man~~ **men** talk.

1. One dogs swims.

2. Two elephant drink water.

3. Three woman eat cake.

4. Many bell ring.

Proofreading Marks	
∧	add
✐	take out

Name _____

Final Blends

Name each picture. Write the letters that stand for the ending sounds. Use the letters from the box.

nd	mp	nt	st	sk

1.

_ _ _ _ _ _ _ _

_____

2.

_ _ _ _ _ _ _ _

_____

3.

_ _ _ _ _ _ _ _

_____

4.

_ _ _ _ _ _ _ _

_____

5.

_ _ _ _ _ _ _ _

_____

6.

_ _ _ _ _ _ _ _

_____

Words to Know

✏️ Write a word from the box to complete each sentence. Use the leftover word to write a sentence.

Words to Know

eat	give	one
put	small	take

_____

1. Liz will _____ Ken a box.

_____

2. He will _____ a snack.

_____

3. I can see _____ duck.

_____

4. The ant is _____ .

_____

5. Jill will _____ the truck away.

_____

_____

135

Final Blends

 Name each picture. Circle the word to finish the sentence.

1.

Fran has a ____ .

list   gift

2.

You can ____ with this.

grasp   print

3.

Ann plays in the ____ .

sand   dust

4.

It can ____ up.

land   jump

5.

Do you sit at a ____?

desk   pond

6.

These can be very ____ .

stand   crisp

Name _____

Spelling Words with the Short *u* Sound

✏️ Write the Spelling Words that end with **un**.

Spelling Words
us
sun
but
fun
bus
run

_____

- - - - - - - - - - - - - - - -

1. _____

_____

- - - - - - - - - - - - - - - -

2. _____

_____

- - - - - - - - - - - - - - - -

3. _____

✏️ Write the Spelling Words that end with **us**.

_____   _____

- - - - - - - - - - - - - -   - - - - - - - - - - - - - - -

4. _____   5. _____

✏️ Write the Spelling Word that ends with **ut**.

_____

- - - - - - - - - - - - - -

6. _____

Articles

 Circle the article in each sentence.
Write it on the line.

1. The gift was a hat.

2. Nan sat at the desk.

3. We stand under an umbrella.

4. The dogs ate fast.

Circle the article that belongs in each sentence.

5. Nan sat on (an, the) steps.

6. He put his bag on (a, an) chair.

Name _____

Writing a Topic Sentence

 Look at the picture of Stan the Skunk.
Tell what Stan looks like. Write a topic
sentence and some details.

Topic Sentence:

_____

- -

_____

_____

- -

He has a _____ .

_____

- -

He has _____ .

Short *u* and Final Blends

Name each picture. Write the last two consonants that stand for the sounds at the end of the word. Choose consonants from the box.

lp	nt	mp	ft	sk

1.

ju _____

2.

a _____

3.

he _____

4.

so _____

5.

bu _____

6.

ma _____

Reader's Guide

A Cupcake Party

Please and Thank You

Read pages 144–149. Help Fritz make a party invitation to give to his friends. Use details from the story to tell about the party.

Please come to my cupcake party!

Where: Fritz's house

When: Today!

What we will do:

_____

_____ .

_____ .

_____ .

_____ .

_____ .

Read pages 150–157. Then be one of Fritz's friends. Write a thank-you note to Fritz. Tell what you liked about the party.

Dear Fritz,

_____

- -

_____

- -

_____

- -

_____

- -

_____

Love,

_____

- -

_____

Name _____

Spelling Words with the Short *u* Sound

✏️ Write the missing letter to complete each Spelling Word. Then write the word.

Spelling Words

us

sun

but

fun

bus

run

_____

1. b ___ t

_____

2. s ___ n

_____

3. ___ s

_____

4. f ___ n

_____

5. b ___ s

_____

6. r ___ n

143

Articles

 Listen to each sentence. Read along.
Circle the article that belongs in each sentence.

1. We went on (a, an) ride.

2. She read about (a, an) elephant.

3. The bear ate (a, the) berries.

4. Bill ate (a, an) orange.

5. I know (the, a) answer.

6. They found (a, an) nest.

Name _____

Spelling Words with the Short *u* Sound

✏️ Write a Spelling Word to complete each sentence.

_____

- - - - - - - - - - - - - - - - -

1. Here comes the _____ .

_____

- - - - - - - - - - - - - - - - -

2. The _____ is up.

_____

- - - - - - - - - - - - - - - - -

3. The dog can _____ fast.

✏️ Write the correct word to complete each sentence.

_____

- - - - - - - - - - - - - - - - -

4. Will you come with _____ ?   **us**

                                                           is

_____

- - - - - - - - - - - - - - - - -   **fun**

5. We had a lot of _____ .   **fan**

_____

- - - - - - - - - - - - - - - - -   **bat**

6. I like black _____ not red.   **but**

Name _____

Spiral Review

🖊 Listen to the words in the boxes. Read along. Write the words from each box to complete each sentence. Use commas and the word *and*.

| dogs   cats   birds |

_____

----

1. We have _____

| sing   dance   act |

_____

----

2. The girl can _____

| apples   plums   pears |

_____

----

3. He eats _____

Grammar in Writing

✏ Write each sentence. Use the article from the Word Bank that belongs in each sentence.

Word Bank

a

an

the

1. My friend has _____ apple.

_____

- -

_____

2. I saw _____ otter at the zoo.

_____

- -

_____

3. The boy has _____ gifts.

_____

- -

_____

Name _____ Date _____

Reader's Guide

From Seed to Pumpkin

My Seed Packet

Make your own pumpkin seed packet.

First, draw a pumpkin plant on the front.

Pumpkin Seeds

Name _____ Date _____

Write about how to grow pumpkins on the back of your packet. Choose words from the box to complete the sentences.

seedlings shoots seeds water flowers

How to Grow a Pumpkin

_____

1. First, plant the _____ in soil.

2. In two weeks, green _____ come up.

3. Next, they grow into _____.

4. Be sure to give your plant _____.

5. In summer, orange _____ bloom on your plants.

6. In fall, you will have big orange pumpkins!

Words with *th*

 Circle the word that matches the picture.

1.

wind   with

2.

tan   thin

3.

them   ten

4.

bat   bath

5.

path   pet

6.

kick   thick

Words to Know

Listen to the riddles. Read along.
Circle the best answer to each riddle.

1. This is a place that is not near.   far   where   live

2. This is how snow feels.   their   blue   cold

3. This word could start a question.   far   where   live

4. A rock does not do this.   cold   where   live

5. Rain is made of this.   water   far   cold

6. The sky is this.   where   blue   little

7. This is not big.   water   little   far

8. This belongs to more than one
person.   their   water   far

Words with *th*

 Write **th** to finish the word and read it.
Circle the picture that matches the word.

1.

$1 + 1 = 2$

m a __ __ __

2.

__ __ __ i n k

3.

__ __ __ i c k

4.

b a __ __ __

5.

__ __ __ i s

Spelling Words with the *th* Sound

Sort the words. Write the correct Spelling Words in each column.

Words that begin with **th**	Words that end with **th**
_____	_____
- - - - - - - - - - -	- - - - - - - - - - -
_____	_____
- - - - - - - - - - -	- - - - - - - - - - -
_____	_____
- - - - - - - - - - -	- - - - - - - - - - -
_____	_____
- - - - - - - - - - -	- - - - - - - - - - -
_____	_____

Spelling Words

that
then
this
them
with
bath

Names for People, Animals, Places, and Things

 Circle each proper noun that names a special person or animal.

1. My friend Kim sees a crab.

2. Stan Bock sees it, too.

3. They call the crab Fred.

 Circle each proper noun that names a special place or thing.

4. We went to the Carson Zoo.

5. We walked from Brown Avenue.

6. My favorite show was Talking Birds.

Words That Tell How

 Draw a sea animal.

```



```

Word Bank

softly
loudly
slowly
quickly
fast
happily
sadly
sleepily
gently

Write sentences about your animal. Listen to the words in the box. Use these words and other words you choose.

Sea Animal	Action Verb	How

Sea Animal	Action Verb	How

Lesson 11
READER'S NOTEBOOK

At Home in the Ocean
Phonics: Base Words and -s, -es,
-ed, -ing

Name _____

Base Words and -s, -es, -ed, -ing

✏️ **Read the sentences. Circle the sentence that tells about the picture.**

1. The cat jumped.

The cat sat.

2. He is helping.

He is resting.

3. She packed a bag.

She pulled a bag.

4. Meg calls her pet.

Meg pets her cat.

5. Val is drawing.

Val is looking.

Reader's Guide

At Home in the Ocean
Interesting Animals

Read pages 16–21. Draw an ocean animal you learned about. Write why it is interesting.

_____

- -

_____

- -

_____.

Read pages 22–29. Draw another ocean animal. Write why it is interesting.

_____

- -

_____

- -

_____

- -

_____ •

At Home in the Ocean
Spelling: Words with *th*

Spelling Words with the *th* Sound

Listen to the clues. Read along. Write the Spelling Word that fits each clue.

_____

1. Rhymes with **cat**   _____

2. Rhymes with **path**   _____

3. Rhymes with **hen**   _____

4. Rhymes with **miss**   _____

5. Rhymes with **hem**   _____

6. Completes this sentence: _____
   I go ___ you.

Titles for People

 Write the titles and names correctly.

_____

1. mrs Scott _____

_____

2. mr Long _____

 Draw a line under each title. Then write the title and name correctly.

3. Today miss Hill will play the drums.

_____

_____

4. Can dr Well fix the dog's leg?

_____

_____

5. ms. Hass takes a picture of the class.

_____

_____

Planning My Sentences

✏️ Write and draw facts about your animal
that lives in the ocean.

My Topic

Fact 1

Fact 2

Spelling Words with the *th* Sound

✏️ Write a Spelling Word from the box to complete each sentence.

Spelling Words

that

bath

them

_____
- - - - - - - - - - - - - - - -

1. _____ hat is for Jack.

_____
- - - - - - - - - - - - - - - -

2. Tell _____ to come in now.

_____
- - - - - - - - - - - - - - - -

3. I like to give my dog a _____ .

✏️ Write a Spelling Word from the box to complete each sentence.

Spelling Words

then

this

with

_____
- - - - - - - - - - - - - - - -

4. _____ Jon was up at bat.

_____
- - - - - - - - - - - - - - - -

5. Matt, is _____ your hat?

_____
- - - - - - - - - - - - - - - -

6. Sam went swimming _____ me.

Spiral Review

✏️ Draw a line under the possessive noun(s) in each sentence.

1. The girl's bike is red.

2. We found Dad's hat.

3. I like Jose's story.

4. The cat's tail is long.

5. This is Miss Linn's book.

Grammar in Writing

Nouns that name special people, animals, places, or things are called **proper nouns**. Proper nouns begin with capital letters.

A **title** before a person's name begins with a capital letter. A title usually ends with a period.

 Fix the mistakes in these statements. Use proofreading marks.

Examples: My fish is named gus.

I gave Mrs Billows a book.

We went to storytime at carter library.

1. My friend dr Rudd helps animals.

2. He has a pet crab called pinch.

3. Our teacher took us to see the liberty bell.

4. We visited the grand canyon.

Proofreading Marks	
∧	add
≡	capital letter

Words with *ch*, *tch*

 Circle the word that matches the picture.

1.

thick   chick

2.

chip   champ

3.

bend   bench

4.

hatch   hut

5.

chin   check

6.

cats   catch

Words to Know

Circle the word that best completes each sentence.

1. The dog is (brown, very).

2. Rich got the gift (been, out) of the box.

3. I would like to have my (never, own) cat.

4. Singing makes me (very, brown) happy.

5. Have you (know, been) to the play?

6. Do you (know, very) what to do next?

7. Take (off, never) that hat.

8. You (own, never) sing with me.

Words with *ch*, *tch*

Read the words in the box. Write the
word that matches the picture.

Word Bank

lunch   check   chimp   chop   match

1.

_____

2.

_____

3.

_____

4.

_____

5.

_____

Spelling Words with the *ch* Sound

Sort the words. Write the correct Spelling Words in each column.

Words that begin with **ch**	Words that end with **ch**

Spelling Words

chin

chop

much

chip

rich

chick

Commands

 Draw a line under each command.

1. Come when I call you.

2. I will call you soon.

3. Run around the track.

4. She can run fast.

 Read each command. Circle the words
this, *that*, *these*, and *those*.

5. Tell those children to come.

6. Eat this apple.

7. Bring me that picture.

8. Sit on these chairs.

Name _____

Order Words

 Write 1, 2, and 3 to put these pictures in order.

 Write instructions that tell how to feed a cat. Use order words.

Order Word	Action	Thing

Order Word	Action	Thing

Order Word	Action	Thing

Name _____

Possessives with 's

✏️ Read the sentences. Circle the sentence that tells about the picture.

1. Mom's hat is off!

Dad's hat is wet.

2. My cat's leg is cut.

My cat's bed is small.

3. Meg's bag is big.

Peg's bag is little.

4. Tim's picture is cold.

Tom's picture is funny.

5. My pal's pet is wet.

The vet is my pet's friend.

Name _____ Date _____

Reader's Guide

Lesson 12
READER'S NOTEBOOK

How Leopard Got His Spots
Independent Reading

How Leopard Got His Spots

Before and After

Read pages 48–59. Draw
one of Fred's friends. What did the friend
look like before and after Fred painted it?
Then write a word to describe the animal
before and after.

Before	**After**

_____   _____

Independent Reading
© Houghton Mifflin Harcourt Publishing Company. All rights reserved.

172

Grade 1, Unit 3

Name _____ Date _____

Lesson 12
READER'S NOTEBOOK

How Leopard Got
His Spots
Independent Reading

Read pages 60–63. Draw a picture of Hal with his new paint job. How do you think Hal feels? Write what Hal might say to Fred.

Spelling Words with *ch*

✏️ Listen to the clues. Read along. Write the Spelling Word that fits each clue.

Spelling Words

- chin
- chop
- much
- chip
- rich
- chick

1. Opposite of **poor**   _____

2. Rhymes with **hop**   _____

3. Rhymes with **fin**   _____

4. Opposite of **little**   _____

5. Rhymes with **hip**   _____

6. Rhymes with **kick**   _____

Name _____

Lesson 12
READER'S NOTEBOOK

How Leopard Got
His Spots
Grammar: Commands

Commands

 Draw a line under each command.

1. We ate dinner.

2. Eat your dinner.

3. Have a snack.

4. She had a snack.

 Write each command to show strong feeling.

5. Wait for me.

_____

- -

_____

6. Hurry up.

_____

- -

_____

Planning My Instructions

Write steps for making an animal puppet. Write the steps in order. Use an order word for each step.

_____
- -

My Topic: How to _____

_____
1. -
_____

_____
2. -
_____

_____
3. -
_____

_____
4. -
_____

Name _____

Spelling Words with the *ch* Sound

✏️ Write the correct word to complete each sentence.

_____

1. Jan rubs her _____ .

_____

2. The _____ is small and soft.

_____

3. How _____ does it cost?

_____

4. Dad will _____ the nuts.

_____

5. There is a _____ in the cup.

_____

6. The king was very _____ .

chin

fin

chick

check

chum

much

chop

chat

ship

chip

rich

rip

Name _____

Spiral Review

✏️ Listen to the animal names in the Word Bank. Read along. Draw lines to match naming parts and action parts. Your sentence should tell about the picture.

Word Bank

zebras   giraffe   turtle

1. The zebras   is hot.

2. A giraffe   drink water.

3. The turtle   has a snack.

4. The sun   takes a swim.

 Write an action part to make a sentence. _____

5. The animals _____.

Name _____

Lesson 12
READER'S NOTEBOOK

How Leopard Got
His Spots
Grammar: Commands

Grammar in Writing

Commands are simple sentences that tell someone to do something. A simple command begins with a **capital letter** and ends with a **period**.

Fix the mistakes in these commands. Use proofreading marks.

Example: <u>w</u>ait for me ⊙

1. feed the giraffe

2. paint a new sign

3. pick up your brush

4. read us this story

Proofreading Marks	
≡	capital letter
⊙	period

Words with *sh*, *wh*, *ph*

Circle the word that matches the picture or belongs in the sentence.

1.

shell   bell

2.

_____

- - - - - - -

_____ is this?

What   Wish

3.

_____

- - - - - - -

_____ will he go?

Well   When

4.

bunch   brush

5.

fish   fist

6.

Ralph   Jen

Words to Know

✏️ Circle the word that best completes each sentence.

1. Some frogs are (green, grow).

2. Let us have lunch (yellow, down) by the pond.

3. It gets cold in the (fall, new).

4. My plants will (down, grow) well in the sun.

5. Some of the buds are (goes, open).

6. Do you like my (new, down) hat?

7. A big (yellow, fall) truck will take the logs away.

8. The truck (green, goes) to the dump.

Words with *sh*, *wh*, *ph*

✏️ Circle the word that finishes the sentence. Then write the word on the line.

1.

wish
witch

_____

I _____ I had a pet dog.

2.

pin
ship

_____

The _____ was in the water.

3.

where
her

_____

Do you know _____ she is?

4.

Then
When

_____

_____ will the shop open?

5.

tan
graph

_____

Dan will draw a math _____ .

Spelling Words with the *sh* and *wh* Sounds

Sort the words. Write the correct Spelling Words in each column.

Words with **sh**	Words with **wh**
_____	_____
_____	_____
_____	_____
_____	_____

Spelling Words

ship

shop

which

when

whip

fish

Write two words that rhyme with **lip.**

_____   _____

_____   _____

Name _____

Subjects and Verbs

 Write a verb from the box to tell what the underlined subject is doing.

Word Bank

pick

hops

sits

run

comes

_____

1. The <u>sun</u> _____ up.

_____

2. <u>Bev</u> _____ on the sand.

_____

3. <u>The girls</u> _____ up sticks.

_____

4. A <u>frog</u> _____ past.

_____

5. The <u>dogs</u> _____ after the rabbits.

Main Idea

Write facts to finish three sentences about a season. Then tell the main idea.

Topic Sentence

Here are some facts about _____ .

Detail Sentence

_____ is a time when _____

_____ .

Detail Sentence

The weather in _____ gets

_____ .

Main Idea

All my sentences tell about _____ .

Contractions with *'s, n't*

Draw a line from each pair of words to its contraction.

can not   don't

Let us   It's

do not   can't

It is   Let's

Write the contraction from above that finishes each sentence.

_____

- - - - - - - - - - - - - - -

1. They _____ know what to do.

_____

- - - - - - - - - - - - - - -

2. _____ good to help a friend.

_____

- - - - - - - - - - - - - - -

3. _____ go to see a play.

_____

- - - - - - - - - - - - - - -

4. He _____ find his hat.

Seasons

Our Seasons

Read pages 82–85. What is important about spring? Draw and write about it.

Spring

_____

_____

_____

_____

_____

_____

Read pages 86–89. What is important about summer? Draw and write about it.

Summer

_____

- -

_____

- -

_____

Read pages 90–97. What is important about fall or winter? Draw and write about it.

_____

- -

_____

_____

- -

_____

Spelling Words with the *sh* and *wh* Sounds

✏️ Write **sh** or **wh** to complete each Spelling Word.

Spelling Words

ship
shop
which
when
whip
fish

1.

___ ___ i p

2.

f i ___ ___

3.

___ ___ o p

4.

___ ___ i c h

5.
January calendar
___ ___ e n

6.

___ ___ i p

Verbs with *s*

🖉 Listen to the nouns in the Word Bank and read along. Choose the correct verb to agree with the underlined subject. Write the verb to finish each sentence.

Word Bank

children   boy   girls

_____

1. Many <u>children</u> _____ by the pond.

play   plays

_____

2. A <u>boy</u> _____ in the water.

jump   jumps

_____

3. The <u>girls</u> _____ the ball.

hit   hits

_____

4. A <u>boy and a dog</u> _____ on the sand.

run   runs

Name _____

Planning My Sentences

 Choose a season. Then write facts about the season.

My Topic: _____

Fact 1

Fact 2

Fact 3

Closing Sentence

© Houghton Mifflin Harcourt Publishing Company. All rights reserved.

Spelling Words with *sh*, *wh*, *ph*

✏️ Write the correct word to complete each sentence.

_____

1. The _____ has left. (shell, ship, chip)

2. _____ way did he go? (Which, Why, Who)

3. The _____ sells hats. (chop, shop, she)

4. _____ will you go? (Where, Went, When)

5. Can you _____ the eggs? (win, why, whip)

6. The _____ are yellow. (dash, fish, dish)

Spiral Review

✏️ Draw lines to match naming parts and action parts. Read the statements you made about the picture.

1. Jill   waters the plants.

2. Fred   takes a nap.

3. The mom   digs in the mud.

4. The dad   is looking.

5. The cat   holds a box of plants.

✏️ Choose one statement. Write it, adding adjectives or other details.

————————————————————————

- -

6. —————————————————————

Grammar in Writing

- Add **s** to a **verb** when it tells about a noun that names one.

- Do not add **s** to a verb when it tells about a noun that names more than one.

 Fix the mistakes in these sentences.
Use proofreading marks.

Examples: Snowflakes ~~falls~~ ^{fall} on the ground.

David ~~put~~ ^{puts} on his coat.

1. Don get his sled.

2. Jan and Nick plays in the sand.

3. Nick make a hill of sand.

4. The dog jump in the grass.

5. Deb and Don finds a cat.

Proofreading Marks	
∧	add
⟋	take out

Words with Long *a*

Circle the word that matches the picture.

1.

camp   crane

2.

plane   plan

3.

crack   cake

4.

grass   gate

5.

whale   what

6.

vest   vase

Words to Know

 Circle the word that best completes each sentence.

1. Can you (watch/into) my fish for me?

2. I will go (into/starts) class with you.

3. I am glad that lunch (watch/starts) at one.

4. The fox jumps (over/watch) the log.

Write the word for each number.

2 _____

3 _____

4 _____

5 _____

> **Words to Know**
>
> five
>
> four
>
> three
>
> two

Words with Long *a*

🖊 Write the word that goes with each clue.

Word Bank

plate
tape
male
skates
game
grape

1. You use this to close a box.

_____

2. A man is this.

_____

3. You eat from this.

_____

4. Go fast on these.

_____

5. This is little and can be green.

_____

6. You play this with a friend.

_____

Spelling Words with the Long *a* Sound

 Write the Spelling Words in ABC order.

_____

1. _____

2. _____

3. _____

4. _____

5. _____

6. _____

Spelling Words

came
make
brave
late
gave
shape

Verbs with *ed*

🖊 Circle the verbs that tell about the past. Write those verbs.

_____
- - - - - - - - - - - - - - - -

1. The game _____ at one.

starts   started

_____
- - - - - - - - - - - - - - - -

2. Stan _____ the box.

fills   filled

_____
- - - - - - - - - - - - - - - -

3. Jane _____ at the pictures.

looks   looked

_____
- - - - - - - - - - - - - - - -

4. The frog _____ very far.

jumps   jumped

_____
- - - - - - - - - - - - - - - -

5. Mr. Scott _____ the best one.

picks   picked

Taking Notes

Listen to this passage about camels. Read along.

Many camels live in deserts. Camels have long legs and humps on their backs. Camels can live to be 50 or even 60 years old. Camels eat plants that grow in the desert.

Take notes about camels. Use words and pictures. Put your notes in the correct boxes.

Bodies

How Long They Live

Food

Words with Soft *c*, *g*, *dge*

✏️ Write the word from the box that rhymes with the set of words.

Word Bank

face
gem
page
cell
judge
wedge

1. fudge   nudge   budge _____

2. cage   wage   rage _____

3. race   lace   pace _____

4. them   hem   stem _____

5. tell   bell   yell _____

6. edge   ledge   hedge _____

The Big Race

Meet the Racers!

Your friend wants to meet Red Lizard and his friends.

Read pages 126–128. What do you know about Red Lizard?

_____

- -

_____ .

Read page 129. Tell about Cottontail.

_____

- -

_____

- -

_____ .

Read page 130. What do you know about Rat?

_____

- -

_____ .

Read pages 131–136. What do you know about Snake?

_____
- -
_____.

Read page 137. Tell about Roadrunner.

_____
- -
_____.

Read pages 138–143. Pick one character to introduce to your friend. Tell important things about the character.

Meet my friend,
_____
- -
_____.

_____
_____
- -
_____
_____

Spelling Words with the Long *a* Sound

 Listen to the clues. Read along. Write the Spelling Word that fits each clue.

Spelling Words

came
make
brave
late
gave
shape

1. Rhymes with **tape** _____

2. Opposite of **afraid** _____

3. Rhymes with **gate** _____

4. Rhymes with **tame** _____

5. Rhymes with **cave** _____

6. Rhymes with **bake** _____

Name _____

Present and Past Time

Listen to the time words in the Word Bank. Read along. Circle the correct verb to show present or past time. Write it on the line.

Word Bank

now   today   yesterday

_____

- -

1. Meg _____ at the clock now. (present time)

looks   looked

_____

- -

2. Today we _____ games for math. (present time)

play   played

_____

- -

3. Yesterday Ron _____ his dad make lunch. (past time)

help   helped

Spelling Words with the Long *a* Sound

Write a Spelling Word from the box to complete each sentence.

came

late

make

brave

shape

gave

_____
- - - - - - - - - - - - - - - - - -

1. I got here _____ .

_____
- - - - - - - - - - - - - - - - - -

2. Will you _____ me a cake?

_____
- - - - - - - - - - - - - - - - - -

3. He _____ to play with me.

_____
- - - - - - - - - - - - - - - - - -

4. Max is big and _____ .

_____
- - - - - - - - - - - - - - - - - -

5. He _____ me a new pen.

_____
- - - - - - - - - - - - - - - - - -

6. What _____ is that box?

Name _____

Spiral Review

Listen to the nouns. Read along. Circle the correct noun to name each picture. Then write the noun.

1.   prize   prizes   _____

2.   child   children   _____

3.   woman   women   _____

Finish the sentence with the correct verb.

4. Plants _____ water to grow.

   needs   need

5. A camel _____ desert plants.

   eat   eats

Planning My Report

Write a question about the animal you choose. Then find and write facts to answer your question.

_____

- -

My Topic: _____

My Question

Fact 1

Fact 2

Fact 3

Grammar in Writing

- Some verbs tell what is happening now. Some verbs tell what happened in the past.
- Add **ed** to most verbs to tell about the past.

✏️ **Listen to the time words in the Word Bank. Read along. Fix the mistakes in these sentences. Use proofreading marks.**

Word Bank

now   yesterday   last night

                              watched
Examples: Many people ~~watch~~ the race
                            ∧
last night.

1. The animals played now.

2. The frog and snake talk yesterday.

3. Last night the rat visits the duck.

Proofreading Marks	
∧	add
℘	take out

Words with Long *i*

 Circle the word that matches the picture.

1.

bake   bike

2.

dime   dim

3.

print   prize

4.

pale   pipe

5.

miss   mice

6.

hive   have

Phonics

Grade 1, Unit 3

Words to Know

✏️ Circle the correct word to complete each sentence.

1. Lan goes for a (walk, bird) in the park.

2. It is a very (both, long) path.

3. Lan sees a (or, bird) in its nest.

4. Will it (fly, long) away when it sees her?

5. Two ducks in the lake are (bird, both) wet.

6. Their (eyes, walk) are black.

7. Lan likes to watch (those, eyes) ducks.

8. Lan has to go now (fly, or) she will be late.

Words with Long *i*

✏️ Write the word that best completes each sentence. Use words from the Word Bank.

Word Bank

time
smile
ride
like
kite

1. Pat and I _____ to play.

2. Pat likes to _____ her bike.

3. I like to fly my _____ .

4. Pat is fun. She makes me _____ .

5. We have a good _____ .

Name _____

Spelling Words with the Long *i* Sound

🖉 Look at the picture. Write the missing letter to complete each Spelling Word.

Spelling Words

drive
time
bike
white
kite
like

1.

t __ m e

2.

l __ k e

3.

k __ t e

4.

b __ k e

5.

w h __ t e

6.

d r __ v e

Using *is* and *are*

 Circle **is** or **are** to finish each sentence. Then write those verbs.

_____

1. The eyes _____ blue.

    is   are

_____

2. The snake _____ thin.

    is   are

_____

3. The chicks _____ soft.

    is   are

_____

4. The mice _____ very little.

    is   are

_____

5. The egg _____ small.

    is   are

Name _____

Using Clear Words

✏️ Listen to the animal names. Read along. Make the meaning of each sentence clearer. Write new words to take the place of the underlined word or words.

1.	A giraffe is <u>big</u>. A giraffe is _____ - - - - - - - - - - - - - - _____ .
2.	Puppies can <u>play</u>. Puppies can _____ - - - - - - - - - - - - - - _____ .
3.	Squirrels can go up <u>tall things</u>. Squirrels can go up _____ - - - - - - - - - - - - - - _____ .

Name _____

Lesson 15
READER'S NOTEBOOK

Digraphs *kn*, *wr*, *gn*, *mb*

Animal Groups
Phonics: Digraphs *kn, wr, gn, mb*

✏️ Circle the two words in each row that begin or end with the same sound. Write the letters that stand for the sound.

kn	wr	gn	mb

1.	wrap	white	wrist	___ ___
2.	lamb	numb	crab	___ ___
3.	kite	knot	knack	___ ___
4.	grape	gnash	gnat	___ ___
5.	write	water	wren	___ ___
6.	knife	knit	kick	___ ___

Animal Groups

What Is an Animal?

Make your own diagram. Look at **Animal Groups** for an example.

Read pages 166–172. Then draw a turtle.

Add labels: scales, tail, eye, legs, shell.

Read pages 173–183. Draw a picture of yourself. Add these labels: hair, eyes, mouth, legs. Add more labels.

Spelling Words with the Long *i* Sound

Spelling Words

time
like
kite
bike
white
drive

✏️ Write the Spelling Words that rhyme with **hike.**

_____   _____

1. _____   2. _____

✏️ Write the Spelling Words that rhyme with **bite.**

_____   _____

3. _____   4. _____

✏️ Write the Spelling Word that rhymes with **dime.**

_____

5. _____

✏️ Write the Spelling Word that rhymes with **hive.**

_____

6. _____

Using *was* and *were*

✏️ Circle **was** or **were** to finish each sentence. Then write the verb on the line.

_____
- - - - - - - - - - - - - - - - - -

1. The cat _____ napping.

was   **were**

_____
- - - - - - - - - - - - - - - - - -

2. The ducks _____ in the pond.

was   **were**

_____
- - - - - - - - - - - - - - - - - -

3. The pigs _____ in their pen.

was   **were**

_____
- - - - - - - - - - - - - - - - - -

4. The snake _____ on the grass.

was   **were**

_____
- - - - - - - - - - - - - - - - - -

5. The frogs _____ in the water.

was   **were**

Spelling Words with the Long *i* Sound

✏️ **Write the correct word to complete each sentence.**

_____
- - - - - - - - - - - - - - - - -

1. I ride my _____ today. (pin, bike, bake)

_____
- - - - - - - - - - - - - - - - -

2. I do not have _____ to chat. (dime, tin, time)

_____
- - - - - - - - - - - - - - - - -

3. I will fly my _____ . (kit, kite, cap)

_____
- - - - - - - - - - - - - - - - -

4. He will _____ the van. (drive, drip, dig)

_____
- - - - - - - - - - - - - - - - -

5. I _____ to read with my dad. (lap, like, lake)

_____
- - - - - - - - - - - - - - - - -

6. He has a _____ hat. (white, bite, what)

Spiral Review

✏️ Write the correct article or demonstrative to complete each sentence.

_____
- - - - - - - - - - - - - -

1. Fish swim in _____ lakes.

a the

_____
- - - - - - - - - - - - - -

2. A fox can hop on _____ log.

a an

_____
- - - - - - - - - - - - - -

3. The bird sat on _____ eggs.

this these

_____
- - - - - - - - - - - - - -

4. We saw _____ otter.

a an

_____
- - - - - - - - - - - - - -

5. The frog ate _____ bug.

that those

Name _____

Lesson 15
READER'S NOTEBOOK

Animal Groups
Grammar: The Verb *be*

Grammar in Writing

- The verbs **is** and **are** tell what is happening now. The verbs **was** and **were** tell what happened in the past.

- Use **is** or **was** with a noun that names one.

✏️ **Fix the mistakes in these sentences. Use proofreading marks.**

Example: Frogs ~~was~~ once tadpoles. A frog
                    ^were   ~~are~~ small.
                                              ^is

1. Cats is mammals.

2. Dogs was once pups.

3. The fox were once a cub.

4. Apes is strong.

Proofreading Marks	
∧	add
و	take out

Reading and Writing Glossary

Use this glossary to help you remember and use words that you are learning about reading and writing.

A

adjective A word that describes a person, an animal, a place, or a thing. An adjective may tell how something looks, tastes, smells, sounds, or feels.

adverb A word that describes a verb. An adverb may tell how, where, when, or how much something is. An adverb may end in -*ly*.

alphabetical order When words are listed in the same order as letters of the alphabet.

antonym A word that means the opposite or nearly the opposite of another word.

apostrophe A punctuation mark (') that takes the place of missing letters in a word.

article A special word, such as *a*, *an*, or *the*, that comes before a noun.

author A person who writes a story.

author's purpose The reason why an author writes a text.

B

....

base word A word to which beginning and ending word parts can be added. A base word is also known as a root word.

biography Informational text that tells about events in a real person's life.

C

....

caption Words that tell about a picture or a photograph.

categorize To name a group of similar things.

category A group of like objects or things.

cause The reason why something happens in a story or text.

chapter book A story that is divided into parts.

characteristic A special quality or trait.

characters The people and animals in a story.

checklist A list of names or things to think about or do.

classify To place similar things in a group.

command A sentence that tells someone to do something. A command can end with a period (.) or an exclamation mark (!).

compare To tell how things are the same.

compound sentence A sentence that is made up of two shorter sentences. The parts of a compound sentence may be connected by words such as *and*, *or*, and *but*.

conclusion A good guess about something the author does not say.

context The words and sentences around a word or phrase that give readers clues to its meaning.

contraction A short way of writing two words using an apostrophe (').

contrast To tell how things are different.

D

....

detail A fact that tells more about the main idea.

dialogue What characters say in a story.

E

....

effect The result of something that happens in a story or text.

entry word A word listed in a dictionary with a definition.

event Something that happens.

exclamation A sentence that shows a strong feeling. An exclamation begins with a capital letter and ends with an exclamation point (!).

F

fable A short story that teaches a lesson.

fairy tale An old story with characters that can do amazing things.

fantasy A type of story that could not happen in real life.

figurative language Words authors use to help a reader picture things in a story. These words may have more than one meaning.

folktale An old story that people have told for many years.

G

glossary A list of words with their definitions, often at the back of a book.

graph A drawing that uses numbers, colors, pictures, or symbols to give information.

graphic features Photos or drawings that stand for ideas or add details in the text.

H

heading A title for a section of a text.

homograph A word that is spelled the same as another word but has a different meaning and may be pronounced differently.

homophone A word that sounds like another word but is spelled differently and has a different meaning.

I

indefinite pronoun A special pronoun, like *anyone*, *everything*, *someone*, *something*, or *everyone*. An indefinite pronoun does not stand for a certain person or thing.

informational text Text that tells about things that are real and contains facts.

informative writing Writing that gives facts about a topic.

M
....

main idea The most important idea about the topic.

multiple-meaning word A word with more than one meaning.

N
....

narrative nonfiction A story that gives information about real people, settings, and events.

narrative writing Writing that tells a story. A narrative tells about something that happened to a person or a character.

narrator The person who tells the story.

noun A word that names a person, an animal, a place, or a thing.

O

onomatopoeia Using words that sound like real noises.

opinion writing Writing that tells what the writer believes and gives reasons.

P

plot The order of events in a story, including the problem and how it is solved.

plural noun A noun that names more than one person, animal, place, or thing. A plural noun usually ends in *-s* or *-es*.

poetry Uses the sounds of words to show pictures and feelings. Poetry sometimes uses rhyming words and other patterns.

possessive noun A noun that shows that one person or animal owns or has something.

possessive pronouns A type of pronoun that shows that something belongs to someone.

predicate The part of a sentence that tells what someone or something does.

prefix A word part attached to the beginning of a base word or root word that changes the word's meaning.

preposition A word that joins with other words to help explain where something is or when it happens.

prepositional phrase A group of words that starts with a preposition.

proper noun A noun that names a special person, animal, place, or thing. A proper noun begins with a capital letter.

Q

question A sentence that asks something. A question begins with a capital letter and ends with a question mark (?).

quotation marks Punctuation marks (" ") that go around the words a character says.

R

realistic fiction A made-up story that could happen in real life.

repetition The same words or same kind of event used over and over in a text.

research report Writing that tells what a writer learned from doing research about a topic.

rhythm A pattern of beats in a poem.

S

sentence A group of words that tells a complete idea.

sequence of events The order in which things happen.

setting When and where a story takes place.

simile Words that tell how two things are the same, using *like* or *as*.

singular noun A noun that names one person, animal, place, or thing.

statement A sentence that tells something. A statement begins with a capital letter and ends with a period (.).

story lesson The lesson a story teaches or its main message.

subject The part of a sentence that tells who or what.

subject pronoun A word that can take the place of a subject, such as *he*, *she*, *it*, *we*, or *they*.

suffix One or more letters that are added to the end of a root word to change the word's meaning.

synonym A word that has the same or almost the same meaning as another word.

T

text and graphic features Photographs, labels, headings, captions, illustrations, dark print, and other special features that add information to a text.

text evidence Clues in the words and pictures that help you figure things out.

thesaurus A book of words in alphabetical order with their synonyms.

topic What a text is mostly about.

V

verb A word that tells what people and animals do.

W

word choice Words writers choose to make their writing clear and interesting, such as words that describe how things look, feel, sound, smell, or taste.